I0253413

I Love You

Inspirational Poetry

by

Sy'needa Penland

Copyright © 2018 by Sy'needa Penland

All rights reserved. No part of this book may be reproduced or trans-mitted in any form or by any means electronic or mechanical, including photocopy, recording or any information storage and retrieval system now known or to be invented, without permission in writing from the publisher. The exception would be in the case of brief quotations embodied in the critical articles or reviews and pages where permission is specifically granted by the publisher. Any members of educational institutions wishing to photocopy part or all of the work for classroom use, or publishers who would like to obtain permission to include in an anthology, should send inquiries to:

Adeenys Publishing,
P. O. Box 716
Dacula, GA 30019
adeenyspublishing@gmail.com

Printed in the United States

Cover design by Sy'needa Penland

ISBN -13: 978-1-942863-07-6

FIRST EDITION

This book is dedicated to the *Spirit of Love.* May it always nourish our hearts.

Contents

A Wonderful Life

No *boundaries.*
No *fear.*
No *hate.*
No *remorse.*
No *chaos.*
No *strife,*

Only the energetic vibration
Of *love*, we create—
Now that's what I consider to be
A wonderful life.

Abundant, Loving Grace

Divine, Mother Universe,
rain down your abundant energy.
Grace thy *earth* with your presence,
for the sake of preserving humanity.

Fill our hearts with your *Divine love,*
from all worlds, *below* and *above*—
May all things, *in-between,* be infused
with your loving *grace,* as old habits
are erased— to bring about unity
of the human race.

May no boundaries exist between us.
Prejudice and hate, shall no longer
divide us. Only *peace* and *love* shall emit
from every dimension of our being.

Adversity

Adversity requires diversity
To evolve into the right
Frame of mind.

When the heart is blind
It will not receive calibration
When cosmic divination
Is bestowed upon thy Earth,
In celebration of *Divine Love*
For thy *Universe.*

May the *GODs* above
Overlook this flaw of hate,
As we celebrate
Your cosmic journey
To soar new galaxies
And sow seeds of *love;*

To cultivate a *Universe*
That is galactically diverse.
As you seal (heal) our hearts,
We shall never depart
From your teachings,
And reaching
For the stars above,
As we resonate the joys of
The Power of Divine Love.

Alpha and Omega

Zenith.
Horizon.
Diamonds.
Crystalline fragments of my *Earth.*

Rebirthed, the *I Am.*
Risen to heal humanity of its curse.
Evil scorned by my loving energy,
which choses to bask in its misery.

Heartbroken from within,
compound with mortal sins.
Hate must create chaos
to fuel one's angry soul.

Lost realm of human fallacies,
allows *all truths* to be told.
As the *Alpha* and *Omega*
rises once more, to collect all debts,
and settle old scores—

To cleanse thy *Earth*
of its ungodly sins,
peace and *love* shall be restored
once again.

Anew

Wake me,
When the *Universe* sings,
For not submitting
To your *demonic reign.*
When she rids *Earth*
Of its evil plague,
Which resurrects itself
During her cosmic mating season—
When all praise and worship
Goes to the *Heavenly Divine,*
Who intertwines all essence
Of thy *Earth* with the rebirth
Of her soul, as she sheds away
The old nature of humanity
And gives rebirth to *Anew.*

Art of Universal Love

Allow me to teach you
Compassion of the heart,
Through creative works of art,
Which requires passion for *love—*
The Art of Giving.

What you will receive
In return, is *love—*
So you must learn to give
Before you receive, *Love.*

Baptize My Soul, in Love

Green pastures,
I lay before you.
Follow the path of the *Divine.*

Open up your soul
To *Mother Earth,*
As she cleanse your mind.

Baptize your *Spirit*
In her essence,
As she cleanse herself of hate.

As she envelopes you
With *Divine Love*,
Loving thoughts,
You shall create.

Blank canvas to her *Universe,*
Each verse of her essence
You shall compose—

Like the petals of a lotus,
New life within
Your *Divine being*
Shall unfold.

Beast Be Gone

Human emotions
Shall be tied to my oceans,
As I absorb source energy.

May my oceans rise,
Beneath my tides,
As I preserve humanity.

Earth is my domain—
Not yours to claim,
With your wicked sorcery—
Beast be gone!

My Earth is no longer
your home,
As I return your soul
To thee—

As thy Universe
Open wide,
To absorb your demise,
My oceans shall
Reflect the beauty
Of my loving energy!

Behold, Truth

Behold, *Truth.*
Mother Universe,
Speak through to my soul
As *Divine Life* unfolds.

Ground thy seed
In your creative essence,
The mystical- magical
Quintessence of you.

Forever guide my *Spirit*
As you ground thy soul,
And inspire all that I do—
In *Truth.*

Black Girls Rock

Black Girls Rock!...
You think not?
My soul neither
Decays or rot.

My soul is as vibrant as
A *Summer's* breeze, in the *Spring*—
I Am the very *essence of life*
That nature brings.

Fruitful is my *Spirit,*
Nourishment is my *Divine soul,*
Like the petals of a lotus,
My *Divine essence* unfolds.

Black Girls Rock!...
You think not?

My hair is as coily
As the *Divine roots*
Of *Mother Earth*—
To *All* life creations,
She gave birth.

My skin,
Like the darkness
Of her fertile volcanic soil,
I harmonize her angelic womb—
I neither hate nor toil.

Black Girls Rock!
You think not?

My natural rhythm
Is in harmony
With the *Divine Universe,*
Who composes the synchronistic
Orchestra of *Mother GOD.*

Healing, is her rod.
Love, is her potion.
As her *Sun* and *Moon*
Balances her oceans.

As new life flourishes
Upon thy *Earthly* shores,
Black Girls Rock!!
Need I say more!...

Black Jade

Black Jade is my shade—
The dark core of thy Earth;
Soulful essence, quintessence
Of thine *Cosmic Universe,*
Who shall lift the curse
From the wretched *Spirit*
Who possesses the soul
Of humanity—

Insanity of a mind
Whose feverish heart
Explodes into the cosmos;
I shall set you free.
As my loving energy
Inspires your *Divine* heart
To love once again.

Black Seed of Life

Theories of creation
Orbits the human mind,
As the naked eye
Is blind to reason.

Long ago,
It was considered treason
To explore the cavity
Of the human soul.

Like the hollow caves
Within thy Earth,
I lie in darkness—

Black Seed of Life,
That nourishes the *soul*
Of humanity.

As *theories* breaches
Thresholds of insanity,
Of human evolution,
The ultimate conclusion
Of life, is *Love.*

Bliss

Emotions,
Feeling,
Love

Happiness
Joy
Pain,
Love

Inspiration,
Motivation,
Rejuvenation,
Love

Love,
The key ingredients
To *Bliss*

Burning Love

Beneath the darkness
Of your majestic seas,
Lies a heart that burns for love.

Ignite my flame this starry night…
Ignite the better half of me…

Do you not hear the cries
Of thy heart— Aching
To be made whole again.

Divine Universe,
Forgive me now
For thy *Earthy* sins—
Ignite the better half of me,
With the essence of *Divinity*.

Calibration of the Soul

Let me make one thing perfectly clear, my dear…
Before I gave *life* its first breathe,
to thrive upon my *Earth*—
was the birth of humanity.
Seeds of life, harvested
within my womb,
the original tomb of death,

Yet to your delight,
you attempt take credit for the birth
of human civilization,
and its vast cultivations,
as you attempt to *bend and flow*
with the energy of "*time,*"
while refusing to take responsibility
for the misbehavior of mankind;

As you wave your guns and forks,
and wage war against my ports,
to threaten my sovereignty—
I shall pause you for a moment or two,
to recalibrate your soul,
as my *Divine Truth* unfolds;
And force you to accept accountability
for what was birthed from you!
To give you one more chance to fix
what is broken with humanity!

Celebration of Life

(Dedicated to the legacy of my beloved grandmother)

A *Celebration of Life*,
is your legacy—
As you hold us
near and dear
to your *Divine Heart,*
for the world to see.

Queen-Monarch,
a pillar of *Divine Life.*
No strife shall come
between those
that you loved,
as your *Heavenly Star*
shines and protect us
from above.

From conception to end,
Alpha and *Omega —Times 3.*
May your *Divine Glory*
cast a *Ray of Hope*,
for *Peace* and *Love*,
for *all* of Humanity.

Cleansed of Sin

Chaotic energy in reverse,
The Karmic curse of mankind—
Eyes blind to my cosmic energy;

Synergy in motion,
The swells of my oceans,
As I heal the pain of humanity;

Eyes shut, now opened wide,
As I pour inside your hearts,
Divine Love.

As below
In-between
Above

I shall cleanse your hearts
Of all you've seen,
As my *Divine Love* balances
And heal thy Earth clean;

All curses broken,
As I leave behind a token,
To pour into your *Divine* hearts—
We shall never part, again.

Cleansed of sin
Cleansed of sin
Cleansed of sin

As I rebirth your souls— Again,
You shall forever be,
Cleansed of sin.

Come Back to Me

Come back to me,
Dear child,
Comeback to me;
Let me cleanse thy soul
With the *Spirit of Love.*
Come back to me.

My waters shall quench your thirst,
Like a burst of fruitful nectars
That blossoms in *Springtime,*
As their roots intertwines
With the top surface of thy *Earth;*

Nourished by the infinite waters
That balances the *sands of times.*
Comeback to me—
Crystalline fragments of thy *Divine Earth*,
Come back to me.

Composition of Love

As the *essence*
Of the *Divine*,
Intertwines
With the
Harmonic sound
Of my voice—
My vibration
Of choice,
My Spirit is
Set free—
To flow
And compose
My thoughts,
In synchronicity
With Earth's
Universal chord
Of soulful,
Loving energy.

Conscience Light

Transformed— My thoughts,
Into the reality of the unknown,
Where the mind of the
Conscience *Spirit* roams.

> *Space,*
> *Matter,*
> *Void.*

It doesn't matter what you call it,
It's all the same—
What matters is what you do with it
When it calls out your name,
To make your final journey
Down the path of *Truth,*
Divine Light— Salvation.

Oh, how the magis of modern-day
Try to teach us to avoid
Traveling down the narrow path
That exists within the boundaries
Of the *conscience light*
That roots our thoughts
To our natural origin,
To appease the intellectual delight.

Solar perplexity of the mind
Blinds the soul to see— Reality,
That's been placed upon the *Spirit*
That does not recognize it—

> *Like kind…*
> *Like mind…*
> *Like energy…*

Yet mind over matter, shatters
All illusions of fallacies.

Cosmic Dance

Cosmic Dance of Ecstasy
Play a tune for me.
Sacred Dance of Divinity,
Transmute loving energy

Within thy soul
New life unfolds,
Replicas of thine Divine-Self;
Truth, ever-lasting.

Cosmic Delights

As creative art explodes within
every fiber of my being,
Cosmic delights of thy *Universe*
is what my *Spirit* is seeing;

When I close my eyes and explore
the multi-dimensions of my mind,
living truth unwinds— reality;

Yet the naked eye is blind to thee—
Cosmic energy, as our airways
are being filled with radio-active,
artificial energy;

Pierce through thy veil,
as her *Divine* story foretells,
what has existed all along…
Love

Cosmic Heart of the Divine

If I could hold
The *Universe* in my heart,
From her *Divine Soul*
I shall never part.
For when she aligns
Her *cosmic* synergy,
I shall receive
And giveth
Loving energy—
Abound
Thy *Earth*
I shall compound
Rebirth,
To reinforce
Her loving veil,
To close the
Pearly Gates of Hell.
As *Divine Souls*
Restores her *Grace,*
Within our hearts
We shall erase,
Remnants of *Earth's*
Wicked past,
At last,
We shall rejoice
In *Love.*

Cosmic Moon

Cosmic Moon,
Pearl of my
Divine Universe,
As you nourish
The soul of thy
Beloved Earth,
So shall you
Rebirth thy souls
Anew—
Your *Divine Guidance*
Shall forever guide
Our *Loving Hearts*
To the center of
Compassion within,
As you cleanse our souls
Of sin—
As the Sunshine
Greats us
At morning light,
Delightful Being
Shall forever crystalize
Thy Beloved Earth,
To balance her soul
Within.

Cover of Darkness

Under the *Cover of Darkness,*
Surrender your soul to thee,
To receive the essence of thine
Universal Energy.

As our souls mate,
To create a *Sea of Divine Love,*
No boundaries shall be set
Between us— Above.

As our hearts anchor to the soul
Of thy beloved *Earth* below,
Within the hearts and souls
Of humanity, *Divinity* is bestowed.

Crystalline Matter

I live in a world
inside my mind.
I live in a place
that was meant to be—
Beyond infinity.

Divine Life,
beyond measure.
Virtual pathway
to the human soul—
Neuro-networks
of crystalline matter.

Dare You Walk Naked?

Unveil yourself to me.
Bare your all, in nudity—
Nudity of the *Spirit*,
Mind, Body, and *Soul.*

Expose yourself to me.
Dare walk naked
Upon my *Earth?*

Dare you revert back to
The basic essentials,
As you once were,
Upon your birth?

When you were first
Introduced to
My wild *queendom.*

When humans walked naked
Amongst the wild.
When they allowed me
To teach and guide
Every mother, father
And child.

Artificial synthetics
Now suffocate the flesh.
Artificial materials
Is where you lay
Your head to rest.

Artificial, fabricated
Dwellings, encapsulates
Your *Spirit* and *mind*,
Thus separating you
From my fertile essence,
As I intertwine—
Reconnect with you,

Along your sojourn
Of modern-day life.

As my *Earthly* nature, yearns to
Reintroduce you to the wild,
Back to the days when you
Embraced me as a child.

Dare you walk naked,
Upon my flesh?
Dare you lay your bosoms
Upon me breasts—

Atop my mountain peaks,
Where my ambiance soothes
Your soul to sleep.
Dare you walk naked?

Dare you walk naked,
To become *One*—
To become whole
With *Mother Earth,*
As you awaken to rebirth,
Dare you walk naked?

Dark Star

For *I AM*
The *first*
And the *last*
Seed of Creation,
Through me—
All manifestations
Of life
Reincarnate
To always be
Part of my
Divine Whole.

Infinite life unfolds
Within each
Fibrous strand
Of my etheric essence,
The All Feeling,
The All Seeing,
The All Being,
Manifestations
Of *Divine Life.*

Darkest Times Fall Gloom

Do you dare try to obliterate my soul—
The very first *seed of life?*
God rested me on thy *Earthly* throne,
To be adorned as the *first wife.*

Many seasons, I have come and gone,
As my *Earthly*-time stands still,
Yet my belly now quakes
As I'm forced to rest the soul
Of thy *free will.*

For human nature has become
To bothersome for me to bear—
Within the depths of the human soul
Lies much anguish and despair.

For misery loves company,
As thy *Divine Love* seeks to prune,
Along your sojourn to wreak havoc
Upon thy *Earth*, under the radiant essence
Of thy *Lunar Moon.*

As my *Sun* rises to the *East* and *West,*
No quest shall come too soon,
For humanity has awaken my inner being,
As the *darkest times fall gloom*

Deliverance of My Soul

(Dedicated to the legacy of my beloved cousin, Ronald L. Carson Sr.)

Family ties, long good-byes,
Deliverance of my soul
Awakens my *Spirit* to *Divine Love.*

I've long awaited this day,
T*he completion of my soul,*
When I can say,
"*Dear Lord, My job is done!*"

As the *Sun* rise and set
On this joyous occasion,
A Great Celebration of Life,
I shall not depart
And leave behind internal strife—
For love is what *I shall leave* each of you.

Let my walk, be your talk,
When you speak of me;
For my legacy is a tough act to follow.
No more pain. No more sorrow.
I shall Rest in Peace!

For this day, shall be a day of
Great remembrance of me,
As I leave you with my final words,
"*I loved each of you, the same!*"

As you glorify his *Holy Name*, *Father God,*
I am ready to return home!
For my *Spirit* shall no longer roam
Thy Earth, I shall return to thee, *A Child of God,*
To be of *Divine* service in your *Heavenly Kingdom.*

Diamond Star

My essence,
Refined—
Like the soul of
Mother Earth.

Composite jewels
Of the *Cosmic Universe,*
Lies upon *her* surface.

Crystalline fragments
Of *her* soul,
Adds a new sparkle
Of *Divine Life.*

Her crystal gems
Adorns the skin,
To warn against
Chaos and strife.

Divine Children of thy Earth

My energetic love tones
Shall ring throughout all dimensions
Of my *Divine Earth.*
Rebirth of my essence
Shall guide the souls of thee,
Divine Children of thy Earth;

Caretaker, is your role
To thy *Universe—*
Great Mother Spirit
Of all *Earthly* creations;

As my harmonic vibrations
Recalibrate the minds of thee,
May you enjoy the riches
Of your *Divinity.*

Divine Life

May the swells of my oceans
forever guide your thoughts
and emotions—

As your *Spirit* flows
with the harmonic vibrations
of my ecstasy.

Energy in motion,
is the force of all emotion,
as life gravitates towards
the *Universal Laws of Divinity.*

Love is the essence of
Divine Life,
which conquers the energy
of chaos and strife—

As *Earth's* heart remains still,
to preserve all life
within her sacred womb.

Infinite, is her vastness.
Divine, is her greatness.
Love, is her essence.

Divine Season of Love

Divine fruits of thou labors,
Nourish thee,
To flourish upon thy Earth.

Rebirthed souls,
Sprouts of your essence.
Springtime is here.

As we rejoice in cheer,
May love be in *season*
Each day of the year.

Divine Seed of Life

As I lay within the comfort
of your *Divine womb*,
a ray of light appears
before me—

Guiding my spirit
to a world unknown,
filled with the majestic beauty
of the Divine Universe.

As *Mother Earth* awakens
me to rebirth,
I will always remember you—
Divine Seed of Life.

Divine Soul

There comes a time in our human lives
When we must seek balance,
To bring *harmony* and *order,* to *light*—
As *Divine Light* shines through to our souls.

As we yearn for peace, love and unity,
Upon our quest for wisdom and knowledge,
Of our *Divine-Self.*

We are told, to first seek permission,
To go forward into the *light,* from a *savior,*
Who religious historians refer to as, *Jesus Christ.*

As historians chronologically detail his path—
His walk with his mother— Often referred to as,
The Black Madonna and Child— We thirst for
The wisdom she poured into her son.

The wisdom and teachings of our mothers
Are never forgotten, but stored within
The sacred chambers of our *Divine Soul.*

The place where darkness meets light—
And become the other half of one's self.
Where *feminine* and *masculine* energy
Is always at foreplay— Seeking to conquer
That of the *Divine Soul.*

Divine Spark of Love

The joys of life, to combat strife,
Is to find a happy medium
To balance *Divine Love* and *hate,*
As we become the manifestation
Of the emotional energy our
Thoughts and actions create—

For compassion grows
The more the *Universe* bestows,
To infuse the human heart
With the *Divine Spark of Love*—
To achieve in the art of
Giving and Receiving.
For in the *Divine* realm,
It's all the same…
L-O-V-E

Divine Thread of Life

The thread that binds us,
To all life's creation;
The Divine essence of thy soul—
Revelation;
Is woven from the sacred roots
Of the Cosmic Universe,
Mystical strands of *Divine* light.

Like the dwarf star that reflects
Its light from *her* heavenly canvas,
The essence of *her Universal* being
Shines through *Earth's* magnificent veil.

Open your heart to receive *her* love,
To fill your hollow soul with the purity
Of *her* fertile essence—
Her crystalline energy of *infinite* grace,
Righteousness, virtue and *Universal love.*

Divinity, is My True Identity

I wear a mask,
To shadow
My true identity.
For I am neither
He or *She.*
I Am, *Divine Energy.*

Born, into flesh,
Re-born into
Neutral skin,
As I walk upon
The top layer
Of thy Earth—
Forced to live
In sin.

To become
Human prey.
To live amongst
Those who desire
My flesh,
Who desire
My soul,
Who desire
My energy.

I wear a mask,
To shadow
My true identity.
Once, risen.
Twice, I rise.
I shall rise above
Those who desire
What I treasure
Inside.

For Divinity
Has touched

My flesh.
As the veil is lifted,
I lift my hands
To the sky,
And ground my roots
To the infinite soul
Of *Mother Earth,*
And give thanks
To the *Great Spirit*,
For my *Rebirth.*

Duty and Service to Humanity

As a devout poet,
I feel that my efforts
Are heroic,
To balance the deeds
Of humanity.

As one's free will
Inspires the will of another,
Let us not forget our duty
And service
To the *Great Mother*—

As caretakers
Of thy *Heavenly Universe,*
Mother Earth.

Dying Breed

Humanity's soul
Becomes weakened
As a collective mass,
And is easier to shatter,
Like broken glass.
Fragmented pieces
of the *Universal Divine Heart*
Shall never part
That of a dying breed—
Whose collective soul
Bleeds upon thy earth,
When returned to thee,
To live on— To infinity.

Earthly Temple

Temple
Of thy *Earth.*
Be it mind
Over matter,
Or thought
Over mind—

The soul
Is never blind
To the
Divine Spirit,
Who is entwined
With the body's
Earthly Temple.

Embryonic Cell of Life

Quite often misconceived.
The strongest emotion
That can either create life
Or destroy it— LOVE.

Energy transformed into living matter.

In the few decades
That I've had the pleasure
To walk upon the *Divine Plains*
Of our *Loving* and *Forgiving*
Earthly pastures,
I've learned that *Love*
Is a kind and gentle *Spirit*
That absorbs the negative
And fearful emotions
Of humanity.

> *As she reciprocates*
> *A harmonic vibration*
> *That resonates from the*
> *Sacred womb*
> *Of Mother Earth—*

Where she rest peacefully.
Undisturbed.
Unpenetrated
By man-kind.
Serenity surrounds her.
As she sleeps peacefully,
Emitting her loving frequency
Through to the *embryonic cell*
Of her Human being.

Creation of life
Requires no explanation
Simply acceptance
Of a *Divine Wisdom,*
That is much higher
Than our own.

Erotic Poetry

Dive right in,
This skin you're in.
While I seduce
Your thoughts
With erotic poetry.
Some say, we were born to sin.

As my words
Penetrate the essence
Below your skin—
Arousing thoughts
Of sensual desire.
Pure ecstasy,
Fuels the fire
Of our passion—
Everlasting, love..

My *Spirit* knows
No gender.
It's neither the giver,
Or sender—
Simply words.
Romantic thoughts.
As your mind, surrender
To my synergy—
The ebb and flow
Of *erotic poetry.*

I welcome you
Into my world of pleasure.
To enjoy my erotic treasures
Of pure ecstasy—
To indulge in
My sensual energy
Of pure delight.
Just say the word.

Essence of Love

Enjoy me,
just as *I Am,*
in this playful
game called lust;

Where rules are
made to be broken;
To surrender your will
is a must;

When skin
embraces skin—
When the energy
of sin—
Is worship.

Like the *Spirits*
of the *Goddesses*
that roam the earth;

Seeking to give birth
to new life—
In the *essence of love.*

Eulogy of Hate

Hate,
May you *Rest in Peace,*
As the *Divine Universe*
Brings about
The perfect balance
Of humanity's sins—

Which begins
With grounding thy soul
In the essence of *Divine Love*
And giving a rose
To the *Spirit of Hate,*
On its sojourn
To its final resting place.

Fearless

Live life
beyond
limitations;
fearlessly.

Young cubs
of the wild,
born a child
of the *Divine*—
all life intertwined.

Earth is your
playground
to run wild
and free.

Free Spirits
is what you
were born to be.

Feminine Essence

What does it mean to be feminine?
Is to awaken the *Goddess* within.
To heal *Mother Earth* of her pain.
To wash away her evil stain.
To balance energy with the rise of the tides.
To give birth to a new *season of Love.*
To old wicked ways, say good-bye.

What does it mean to be feminine?
To be the *Mother* of civilizations,
As they *rise,* and *fall*—
To give praise to the *Divine Creator,*
Who created it all.

To know our rightful place in this realm;
The *Earthly Star* beyond the horizon.
As she bask in the *Glory of the Universe*,
Beneath the crescent *Moon* and the *Sun*,
Is to know that our work is never done.

Flame of Love

Heaven's gate
To the eternal hell
Of thy soul,
Passion fueled
By desires of thy flesh.

Once was,
Now delivered
To your *Divine Light,*
Our *Flame of Love*
Never burns out.

For the Love of Thy Earth

Gates of Hell,
Where the soul of hate prefers to dwell,
Open up your chambers this night—
Welcome its old *hateful-spirit* home.

Upon thy *Earth,* it shall no longer roam,
As the *Spirit of Love* greets us at morning light;
Our worlds shall be forever divided,
As *Heaven* and *Earth* are united.

We shall part in the name of *Peace,*
Love, and *Compassion*
For thy beloved *Universe.*

Forever Bond, in Love

Deep within my soul,
I will always treasure
My love for you.

You are the air
To my every breath,
You inspire all that I say
And do.

You are the very definition of *Love,*
Which leaves no empty void
In my heart.

Our union is *forever bond, in Love*
And nothing
Shall tear us apart.

Fragmented Pieces of Life

Silenced voices
Beckons me
To the wild—

Somber cries.
Once tormented flesh.
Bodies maimed
Before their death.

Washed upon the shores
Of my sacred creeks.
Remnants of life,
Once vibrant and free;

What remains
Of the fragmented pieces—
A life shamed
In misery.

Free Will

By the powers invested
In thy *Holy Name,*
I ask for your forgiveness;
For our lives to be the same.

We shall never part
From your *Divine* teachings,
As you seek to calibrate
The moral compass
Of thy *free will.*

Through my quill,
I shall lend
To the essence of
The *Great Divine,*
To help mend
Humanity's
Broken heart.

As all life entwines
With thee,
Your devout love
Bestows synchronicity
Within thy core,
As *Peace, Love,*
And Goodwill
Upon thy *Earth,*
Is restored— *Once more.*

Fruitful Earth

I woke up this morning,
feeling a peculiar kind of way,
I said, *Devil, it's nice to meet you,*
have a seat, why don't you stay?

As he returned the smile,
agreeing to stay for a while,
I offered him a cup of tea and said,
I'm headed outdoors, why don't you join me.

Grabbing his bag of tricks,
a quick glimpse, I did not miss.
He reached for my hand,
and offered me a kiss.

What a gentleman, so full of charm.
Yet he's known to do you harm.
I politely extended him my arm,
as he embraced me by his side,
agreeing to accompany me outside.

He reached for the handle on the door,
once more, a gentleman.
In complete disbelief,
known for his mischief;
I also reached for the handle on the door.

Greeting us with her delightful smile,
Mother Earth's radiant beauty
stretched for miles—
We both agreed to sit a while.

One by one,
the blossoms began to sprout.
As the trees began to shout,
"Thank God he's here!",
they sang in harmonic cheer.

Dazed and confused,
I was suddenly infused
with a burst of energy.

Divinity, was all around,
bestowed upon her *Holy* ground,
our *Spirits* became compound
with *Mother Earth.*

Rebirthed, my *Angels,*
as I unite the two of you
to live as *One body,* and *soul.*

As I remold thee,
into the likeness of me,
may your essence conjoin as *One*,
in union under the *Sun*;

Rebirthed into the likeness of
the *Cosmic Universe.*
I rebirth your souls anew,
to live a fruitful and abundant life.

No more living divided
in a world of strife—
You are hereby anointed
in the name of the, *I Am.*

As *above*,
So *below*,
In-between
All things shall be, of me!

Georgia's Clay

Oh, broken down
Georgia's clay,
That deeply nourishes
My soul—
As the essence
Of your minerals
Unfolds within.

Each delicate layer
Of your ore,
Refined to its purest,
Invigorates my skin,
As the blood
Of the oceans
Washes ashore.

Oh, how I love to
Feel you…
Till you…
Mold you…
As you bleed
The very richness
That nourishes me,
As I welcome
The beauty
Of your essence,
Divinity.

GOD's Grace

May the Energy of
Love,
Peace,
Justice,
Unity,
Respect,
Kindness,
Compassion,
Tolerance,
Patience,
Balance,
Harmony,
Forgiveness,
Caring,
Sharing,
Good Will,
Synchronicity,
Reciprocity in Kind,
Obedience to the Universe,
Divine Protection of all *Living Beings,*
And GOD's Grace,
Be bestowed upon humanity,
In the Name of thee,
Great Mother, Divine Universe.

Greater Good

As compassion grounds your soul,
May the *Spirit of Love,* fuel your energy,
To be of higher service to others,
In the *Name of Divinity*

Be of righteous mind.
Be wise with your words.
Be firm in your talk.
Be strong in your walk.

Be brave along your path.
Be humble and fearless,
As you compromise in your service,
For the greater good.

Guide My Soul to Freedom

Black raven in the mist,
Guide my soul to freedom.
Wandering, I shall be no more;
Washed upon the shores of shame—

As darkness falls, the sun shall rise again
To guide the way amidst the wind;
I shall soar upon the open seas,
As my *Divine Spirit* is set free.

Healed of Sin

The healing light
Shall guide your paths,
For my *Spirit* shall not
Overshadow thee.

Lunar Moon,
Guide my beloved *Spirits*
Home— Upon thy *Earth*
They shall no longer roam.

Spirits called forth
To do bad deeds,
Has plagued the realm
Of humanity—

Thy heavenly *Earth*
Has not forsaken thee,
As the *Universe* cleanse
The soul of thee;

She shall welcome you home
Once again—
As her *Earthly* beings
Are healed of sin.

Heart and Soul of Humanity

For *I AM* the Divine
Poet Laureate,
As *Universal Love*
Flows through the artisan
Of my quill,
As I surrender
My *free will*
To receive
Divinity,
As my eyes awaken
To reality,
As an obedient scribe
Of modern times.

As the Universe
Entwines
Truth
In all
I say and do,
I shall remain
A righteous soul,
As the forces
Of positive and negative
Polarities unfolds
To bring about unity
Of love
Within the heart and soul
Of humanity.
For I shall not allow
The human mind
To be labeled
As *insanity*
Or feeble minded,
As the veil
Is being reinforced
To keep the Spirit blinded
To receive love and Divinity.

Heart of Steel

Magic sorcery embody me,
Heal me this very night.
Under the moonlight,
I stand beneath thy *Lunar Goddess,*
To receive your loving essence.

Immortal soul of thy *Universe,*
I am healed— *Heart of steel.*
I shall go forth and champion
The preservation of humanity,
For *Peace* and *Love* upon thy *Earth*
Once again.

Heavenly Body of Thy Earth

Divine Rapture;
As my Spirit,
Mind, Body
Awakens me to *Love.*

Divine union of the
Halves of my soul,
Made whole
By the *Divinity* above,

For I come together
In *Peace,*
With the *Heavenly Body*
of thy Earth;

As her star shines bright,
For all of the *Universe* to see,
As she rises to the occasion
Of *Infinity*—

May the fertile union
Of all of her *Divine Species*
Be nourished by the cosmos,
Now and forever more.

House of Dreams

Pierce your *loving* eyes
Through to my tender heart.
Awaken my *Spirit*
With your *Divine Spark*—
Kindred souls,
Passersbys, in our lonely lives.

Meet me in paradise.
In our house of dreams,
Made into reality—
Here we are, again.

How Do We Manifest Love

How do we manifest *love*
Into the realm of our daily lives
That is so filled with the energy of hate
That's become the living reality
Of the actions we create?

Mind-controlled warfare,
In an elitists' world of fear—
Afraid that one day
They will be empowered by
What the *Universe* holds dear.

A compassionate *Spirit*
Does not measure material wealth
Or success, but encourages
Kindness and gratitude—
To do our very best.

Compassion and *Peace*
Laid root on a *loving* foundation,
Are the strongest building blocks
Of life, from conception to birth,
As it nourishes each phase
Of our daily lives.

Human Nature

Allow me to explore the minds
Of *freewill* thinkers,
The great *magis* of modern times,
Who seek to rewind, and intertwine
Our thoughts and behaviors,
To prove that his*(her)* theories
Are more convincing
Than that of another;

As if the *Great Mother Spirit*
Would not intervene to hear it—
Free thoughts of the thinker,
As she allows *free will*—
Human nature,
To flow with the essence
Of her *Divine will.*

Take my *quill* for instance,
As a devout *Sage* of the *Divine*,
Who entwines my thoughts
With her will, as my quill
Flows with the essence
Of her *Divine* heart—
For we shall never part.

Since the conception of my birth,
When she rebirthed herself
In the essence of my soul,
Divine Life began to unfold
Within my being,
As she guides my thoughts
In believing in her *Divine will.*

As human nature evolves,
For it shall breathe,
Expand and become
The better half of thee,
Divinity—

Makers and creators of *Divine Life,*
Who thrives upon thy *Earth.*

Upon rebirth, the *Divine*
Gives nourishment to each of us
The same, as we evolve
To restore her *Divine Essence,*
In the name, of *Love.*

Humanity's Curse

For *I AM*
The *darkness*
Who sees the *light,*
Through my eyes
I give you sight;

In all realms
You shall see,
The beauty
Of my mystery;

As glory from thy
Heavens, shines
Upon the soul
Of thy *Universe—*

I lift the artificial veil,
To break humanity's curse.
Deeds of the past
Shall not meet its untimely fate,

As the vibration of love
Becomes the synchronistic rhythm
Our soul creates.

As time stands still
From the very flow of my quill,
For I shall never surrender
Thy free will,
But only to *Love.*

I AM, GOD

The *Universe,*
Broke the mold
When I was sold
Into slavery,
Mental, that is.
Yet these hands
Have never
Been shackled,
Neither have these feet.

I have walked
A thousand miles
Upon thy *Earth,*
As she stands beneath
My blackened feet.
My feet have touched
The darkest soil—
My soul, tormented,
As my mind toils
With the *idea of slavery?*

For I have birthed
The strongest man
Known to human kind,
Whose soul is blind
To your sorcery.
I will dig a grave
And bury you,
Before I surrender
To your mental captivity.
For I AM *GOD,*
A Child of the Universe,
I AM.

I Am Ready to Surrender

Love,
Do not challenge me,
For I am ready to surrender
To your will—

As my heart stands still
To receive your energetic vibrations
Through my quill,
I vow to be forever faithful
To your *Divine Essence.*

I Give Birth to Poetry

With each rhyme and meter
of my poetic verse,
I give birth, to poetry...

As my *Essence* flows
with the iambic pentameter
of the *Universe,*
I give birth, to poetry...

Curses broken
with each word spoken,
a token of *Divine* love,
I give to humanity...

Poetry is my *craft* of choice,
as I lift my gifted voice,
and give hope to thee…

As I apply rhyme to reason,
in each new season, of love,
I give birth, to poetry.

I Lay Down My Soul

Dear Lord,
I lay down my soul, beside you.
As I sleep, a thousand nights.
As I dream, a thousand thoughts.

I lay down beside you—
Seeking, Eternal Peace.

Rest me,
In comfort, Dear Lord.
In the bosom of *The Great Divine.*

Rest me,
In your *Cosmic Heavens,*
Beyond your *Earthly Star.*

I Love You

I shall paint a portrait of *LOVE*
Across my *Earthly* sky—
A reflection of my *inner soul.*
Like a soothing lullaby.
Each day you see reflections
Of *my Divine Love* for humanity,
My *loving essence* shall resonate
From the soul of your *Divine Spirit,*
Til infinity.

Imagine…
    Seeing,
    Hearing,
    Feeling,
    Being
The words, *I Love You…*

Each time you gaze upon
My heavenly portrait—
As my soulful vibration,
I Love You,
Echoes through to your
Heart's center.
As you *Become*
A mirrored reflection
Of my *Divine Soul.*

I Return to You

In the solitude of silence
I return to you,
The guiding light
That pierces through
The darkness
Of a broken soul.

Prayers lifted
With each breath,
You take in me—
Divinity
Of the human *Spirit,*
Which carries
The flame of love
In the wind.

As I return to you
Whole,
No longer
Fragmented pieces
Of the *Divine*
But that of flesh
That has risen
To the sanctuary
Of the heavens;

Angelic beings,
Who walk upon thy Earth
To share wisdom
Of thy kingdom of heaven
Which resides within
The Earthly heart
Of the human soul.

I Submit to You

Your lustful aroma
is as alluring as your smile,
as it captivates my *Spirit*—
Your *Soul* beckons me
to stay awhile.

Your feminine beauty,
weakens my masculine heart—
Twin souls torn apart,
united in the *essence* of love,
once again.

Love is the harmonic melody
of our conjoined hearts,
beating in rhythm as one.

I submit to you,
My Queen,
My Deity of Love—
I submit to you,
My Divine.

Tonight we shall dine
along your fertile *Nile,*
under the crescent *Moon,*
as the glory of the *Sun*
forever bond our hearts—
We shall never part.

I'm Drownin, Rescue Me

I'm drowin,
rescue me,
I can't run—
there is nowhere
to hide.

The tides are high,
I'm drownin
in a sea of love.

I can't save myself,
the pain is surreal,
I can't feel
my emotions—
I'm drowin
in an ocean
of love.

As my emotions
pours into the sea,
my Spirit screams, *rescue me,*
I'm drownin in a sea of love.

Immaculate Conception of the Universe

When pain becomes pleasure,
  And two souls are forced to measure
One's happiness, over the submission
  Of the other—

When, *"Surrender your free-will to me,"*
  Is chanted during that moment of ecstasy,
And the *Loving Spirit* of the *Divine* is drawn to
  The beating heart of thy another—

When passion intertwines loving beings,
  Masculine and *Feminine* energy,
And *Divine Love* is poured into their souls,
  As *Divine* conception unfolds,
And the *seed of life* is nourished by
  Immaculate Conception of the Universe.

In the Name of Love

I shall call your name,
I shall glorify you,
I shall magnify you,
My Lord, Creator,
I shall embody you.

Master of creation
Of all denominations,
Bring forth liberation
Of my soul.

Master of my will,
Art of my quill,
Stroke of my pen,
Were love begins.

Omnipotent energy,
Synergy of all around.

With each breathe—
    I shall manifest you.

With each stroke—
    I shall manifest you.

With each thought—
    I shall manifest you.

With each word spoken—
    I shall deliver you,
        In the name of Love.

Joy, Love, and the Good Life

Joy, Love and the Good Life,
Shall be the manifestation
Of loving energy,
From the positive thoughts
I create;

To show that I appreciate
A life worth living,
With giving absolute LOVE,
And spreading seeds joy
To each life form
I encounter;

Nothing else matters
But the good times
In life—
Whatever that may be.

Justice, Ordained

Children of thy *Universe,*
As all life entwines with thee,
Ordained within your souls,
Divine, *Loving Energy;*

Peace bestowed,
Unto a heart scorned—
Bullied by social norms;

You are ordained with equality,
As the *Scales of Justice*
Balances all life within thy Earth;

Rebirth of all mankind.
No longer blind to thee.
As Root Culture
Fill your hearts with everlasting
Satisfaction—
Peaceful and *Loving Energy.*

Kindred Spirits

As the kindred *Spirit of Love*
Envelopes my soul,
I surrender to *Divinity*—
The *Essence of Life,*
The *Great Mother*
Of all creations—
I surrender my all,
As love magnifies my *Spirit,*
Mind, Body and *Soul,*
I become whole.

Let Me Rest in Peace

Wake me up when it's over.
Like the rover that explored
Beyond *Earth's Universe,*
Testing the boundaries
Beyond matter—
Life shattered.
Spells casted against me.
Curses broken.

I leave behind a token
Of *love,*
As my *Spirit* soars above—
High in flight,
Eagle landing
On the moon,
Not a day too soon,
I arrive back on *Earth.*

Rebirthed, at the sound
Of a quake, I'm awake.
Awoken from the hell
You stuck in.
New life begins, again,
When new life forms—
Reborn, to not conform
With society's norms.

Christian, I am not.
Guess you forgot
Who *I Am.*
Not a son of *Uncle Sam.*
Benjamin don't own me.
He never bought me.
Free…
I was born to be!

Music in my soul.
Music in my bones.

Music in my *roots*,
As I write the lyrics
To this poetic song.
My *Earth*— Compound.
My *roots* are sound,
Never torn from the *Earth,*
Never uprooted from her
Divine soul.

My *Spirit* don't toil with anger.
My *Spirit* don't run
At the sight of danger.
I Am a warrior!
Love is what I fight for!
Love is what I was born for!
Love is who *I Am!*

Wake me up
When you want to feel *Love*.
Until then, let me rest in peace…

Life Force Energy

Balanced emotions.
As my *Spirit* flows
With the mystic tides
Of thy oceans—
Sacred Womb of Divine life.

Heavens above meets
Heavens below,
As the essence of
Divine life is bestowed.

Enriched, thy *Earth,*
As her roots extends
To the *Divine Universe,*
To nourish the souls of
Humanity.

As I intertwine your souls
with the soul of thy *Earth,*
I shall incarnate you
into the likeness of the *I Am.*

Etheric coils— fibrous strands
of *Divine Life*, woven within
Life Force Energy—
Galactic beings of thy *Universe.*

Life's Pleasures

Life beyond measure, is a pleasure
for someone living an extraordinary life.
When temptation introduces you to sin,
as your moral compass is at strife
with the *Spirit* that calibrates the *Soul* within.

Outer and inner worlds collide,
as negative entities seek to divide
your house, when the *Divine Universe*
reinforces your soul's foundation,
to avoid confrontation—
As you resort your thoughts
back to an ordinary life.

Go have some fun, under the *Sun,*
where pain and pleasure go to play.
"Take in all of me," says, *Divine Energy*,
as she rejuvenates our everyday lives,
with the essence of *solar energy.*

Living Legacy

(Dedicated to the memory of my late cousin, Ron L. Carson)

As death awakens my *Spirit,* I shall light a candle for you,
To ground your *Spirit,* and guide the way for you.
If there was ever a soul that left us to soon,
Cuz, That soul was you!

The last words that we spoke were, I love you.
Just yesterday, when I heard your voice,
Little did I know that the *Universe* was making her choice,
To allow your *Spirit* to soar amongst the *Angels,*
As a *Guardian* to those you leave behind.

For their hearts shall not be blind to your *Divine Energy,*
As you give them unconditional love, in synchronicity
With the *Divine Universe.*

As Earth is to Earth—
You shall be rebirthed;
As Fire is to Air—
Your *Spirit* shall be everywhere;
As Water is to your Divine Soul—
Your reincarnation shall be as bold as the mighty lion—

Your *Sun* shall rise, as high as the heavenly skies,
Conjoined with the *Divine Universe;*
Your *Spirit* shall always be forever grounded
To thy beloved *Mother Earth!!*

Love Conquers Hate

We can remove *Flags*
and *Monuments* all day,
but what will it take
to make the pain go away?

Hate in a man's soul,
reveals buried *Truths* untold;
Anguished *Spirits* never rest—
Unleashed is the pain of *self-misery*;

His failure to reshape the *world*
into what he thinks it ought to be;
His failure to be better than
the next man— One who's skin
is as dark as night;

Bearing the resemblance of
the canvas that reflects his
heavenly stars at night,
as he's proven to himself,
time and again, for centuries,
that *black don't crack;*

The *black-back* that has survived
the brutal lashes of his oppressor—
Evident in the gifts and talents
of his *new-born* seeds;

His sons now *OWN* the gridiron,
as if he invented the game called *Football*,
that is systematically designed
to profit from his labors;

As centuries-long past, the enslaved
mind, body and *Spirit,* is once again
a *Slave* to his choices in life,
while he's paid handsomely to lead

the charge of the next generation;
As they are herded like cattle to be
the next *Jim Crow* that will never fly
like the Eagle, but will leap across
the in-zone and score points
on a scoreboard—

While *bets* are made, and paid,
as new strategies are being designed
to build larger coliseums to display
"The best of the best" amongst
the mascots of the wild kingdom;

If only *Love* was poured into
the hearts and minds of our children,
maybe… Just maybe… We can produce
an enlightened generation of *Monks*
or *Spiritual Gurus*, to lead the charge…
Who knows, but in the end,
Love Conquers Hate!

Love is at Peace, With Itself

Love is at peace with itself,
It doesn't need validation.
It is Divine confirmation of infinity,
Life lived, many times over.

It's a life that's been hurt many times over.
It's a life that's been healed many times over.
Love is at peace with itself,
It doesn't need clarification.

For love emits its own energy,
A synchronistic vibration of itself,
A harmonic, rhythmic vibration of itself,
A *Divine Reflection* of itself.

Love is at peace with itself,
It doesn't need a standing ovation,
Praise for its Divine existence,
Or a hallelujah, or thank you, *Jesus.*

Love is at peace with itself,
It doesn't need competition
From false sources of Divine energy.

Love is *100%* pure and natural energy,
Gifted from the *Cosmic Universe,*
Creator of all life— Sustainer of all living beings.
For *love* is life, and life is *love.*

Love is at peace with itself

Love Spell

If I could cast a spell,
I would shower
The *Universe* with love—
As many spells
That it would take,
To break the spell of hate—
So we can become
The positive energy
Of the *loving* essence
We create.

And the Universe replies,
"It shall be done!"

Loving Star

Heavenly Dimensions
Unite as one,
Under the celestial body
Of thy sun.

Star galaxies, far away,
From thine hearts
You shall not stray,

Too far
From thy beloved *Earth,*
Where the naked eye
Cannot see—

Infuse thy soul with
Divine, loving energy.

As the moon,
Rise and sets,
I shall receive all that you
Have to give—

As a *loving conduit*
Of thou beloved *Earth,*
For as long as I shall live.

As she rebirths
The soul of creation,
My celestial being
Shall have no limitations;

As you create the
Greatest manifestation,
Of our modern-day times.

Majestic Creations

"Am I not the one who gave you life?,"
Wept the dying words of the *Universe's*
First wife, before *she* reincarnated
Her essence to become the *sacred jewel*
Of *thy* earth.

Rebirthed *Stars,*
Fragmented crystals,
Galaxies of forbidden love—
Torn apart, *her* broken heart,
By the other half of *her* broken soul;

Made whole, *her* earth,
As she protects *her* sacred womb;
The chamber of eternal life;

She shall never part
Her majestic creations—
Fibrous strands of *Divine* life,
That connects thy souls
to the core of *her* etheric earth;

As *she* nourishes all life
Within her *Divine* essence,
To harvest thy souls for rebirth,
May we evolve in the *Spirit of Love.*

Matrimonial Love

Must I stare into your wicked soul,
as *Divine* life flourishes within.
For hate is desperate to receive my love,
to cleanse itself of sin.

Dare hate stare into my loving eyes?
Perfect, our union— A match made in heaven.
Let us join our *Divine* souls in matrimonial love.

Mirrored Reflections of My Soul

Everyone has a journey,
we all have a story to tell;
When the soul needs to
release a thought,
the *Spirit* often yells,
"*Dear Lord, rescue me from pain,*
so I can breathe again—

So my eyes can see past the
mirrored reflections of my soul,
which basks in self-misery.
As I overcome trials and tribulations,
my flesh is set free— from the energy
that entangles my *Spirit*—
I become released from captivity.

My Dearest America

My Dearest, America,
Do not weep for me,
As you celebrate my legacy.

For I have left behind
Proud sons, who will continue to
Pave the way.

For they are their father's sons
Who have proven that the job
Will get done!

As they were groomed to stay
One step ahead.
The game is not over,
Until I say it's over.

So boys, carry this nation
Full speed ahead!
Forever yours,
Divine Universe

My Other Half is You

A plethora of lies, is where your plight begins,
as you continue to retrace your roots, to mankind's
original sin— Which is said to be where religious
heritage begins;

As wicked sorcery pours through to the human soul,
Divine life unfolds— Deeply rooted within the essence
of your skin, the origin of my existence begins;

As I rebirth your souls a new, I shall lift the curse,
placed upon your birth, as you enjoy the nectar of my
plentiful Earth;

No more suppression of the mind— Eyes no longer
blinded by fallacies— As I lift the veil to reveal my truth,
you shall come to understand that my other half, is you.

Native Spirit

Native sparrow, to the cause;
My *Spirit* shall not defy the laws
Of human nature—

At free will, others will
Infringe upon thy quill,
While seeking to soar like an eagle
To protect the young
They have borne—

Don't be scorned by their wicked ways,
For the *Universe* shall guide the way
To be of *Divine service* each day.

Nature's Spirit

Don't underestimate yourself
By overestimating yourself.
Life is full of challenges
With pitfalls along the way.

Before you seek to conquer
Your destiny, get a lay of the land,
Connect with nature— *Mother Earth's*
Natural environment, and let her
Spirit guide you along life's journey.

No More Wars

When are we going to open our eyes to see
that violence is not the solution to solve
the problems of humanity—
Love is the cure for all *sadness*,
all chaotic *madness*, and will bring about
peace and *gladness*, within the human heart.

No More Wars,
As our villages are torn apart.
As our lives are ripped apart.
As our hearts are cut open,
to become *auctioned* body parts.

No More Wars,
As the collective consciousness fight to
open doors within the human hearts
and minds, that are no longer blind
by illusions of *Truth*—
When the reality of *Truth,* is that
we were born of *Source energy.*

Not energy derived from "*artificial intelligence.*"

Soon, you will come to realize
that the programmed hackers
are the *true attackers* of consciousness.
Yet they themselves believe the lies
that they are the *genius minds*
who remain blind to the hypocrisy
of science, who profess itself to be
the foundation of all creations.

As the Book of Revelations unfolds,
Truth shall be told!!

Yet WE, the *collective consciousness*
are in fact, the *True God Force Energy*,
working in synchronicity—

As *Galactic Orbital Dynamics*, aka *GOD*,
which keeps the world spinning.

Yet the energy of the sinning *flesh,*
seeks to attract and devour
the flesh of another, which seeks to
stake claim to the rightful inheritance
of thy brother.

So goes the story of *Cain and Able.*

Yet the mythical beliefs— manmade fallacies,
directs energy towards the notion that
"*my skin*" is better than "*your skin*,"
but in reality "*my skin*" is the *skin*
that commits the worse sins,
Cardinal Sins, I must add.

It's a sad-day in modern-day reality
that *WE STILL CAN'T GET ALONG*—
Shall be the song that is praised to the
Most High Angels, as they seek a better way
to save humanity... From ourselves.

Obedient Scribe for the Universe

No thoughts, rhyme,
or reason, comes to mind,
as I stare at a blank page of life.
Releasing the essence of my
emotions, from the cruelty
of humanity's strife.

I've arrived at the end
of this remarkable journey,
as a seasoned- devout *Sage.*
Many words I've stroked
with my pen, penetrating
the veil of humanity's sins—
Discovering the secret origin
of where human life begins.

Crossing dimensional
boundaries, only to see
the other side of reality—
Truth beyond the hidden veil,
is what the energy of
the *Great Spirit* foretells.

Time — Space — Delusions
Implanted illusions within
the human mind. Eyes shut,
opened wide, I've crossed over
to the other side. Reality—
Hypocrisy, it's all the same to me.
Obedient Scribe for the Universe,
shall read the marker of *my legacy.*

One Earth

I love you
Like the *moon*
That shines down
On my *Earthly* face.

I love you
Like the *sun*
That shines its rays
To energize my heart.

May our *love*
Forever bond,
And nothing shall
Tear us apart;

Twin Hearts.
One Soul.
One Earth.

Past Virtues

If you wish to have thy *Earth*
Cleansed of hate—
Evil shall exist no more.
Old scores settled!

Revenge shall be a sin
Of the past, forgiven by
Divine Love.

As humanity evolves into a much
Kinder and gentler race,
Grace shall be your guide—

To evolve in love and compassion,
Within the *Universal being*
Of thy planet *Earth.*

Peace and Love

Sing to me,
O' Morning Glory,
as I bask in your delight
this peaceful day.

Sun light sparkles,
raindrops glistens,
as the tulips sway.

Gentle breeze
beneath my wings,
as you carry me
through the air;

As I spread
the delightful essence
of *Peace* and *Love*
everywhere.

Peace Offering

The fruit of thy *Earth*
Is Compassion—
Rebirth of the *Divine Soul.*

Love is my peace offering to hate,
As its energy creates
More destructive vices
To destroy humanity.

What did I do to deserve this?,
Cries the *Universe,* but love you.

Poetic Wisdom

Wisdom and understanding
comes to me naturally,
As I connect my mind and soul
to *Divine* energy.

Channeler of the *Divine,*
my meter keeps no time.
Conduit of the *Universe,*
whose energy flows through
each poetic verse.

Pen, is my instrument of choice,
as I scribe the essence of
her poetic voice.

Creativity is my art,
as my spoken word pours
loving energy of the *Divine*
into your hearts and minds.

Potion of Love

Crafting words is my potion,
as I flow with the harmonic
vibrations of life.

Each word spoken
brings *Divine Energy*
to my oceans;

As I nourish and mend
Earth's broken seeds,
from strife.

Divide and conquer
once more, as hate fuels
the burning flame of
Earth's core.

My waters shall
soothe her soul,
as new life unfolds,
as history is retold.
Again and again.

As *Divine* souls
are cleansed of sins—
As we repeat this journey,
again…
I shall spell you
in the *name of love*

Power of the Hour

Power of the Hour,
Come rescue me,
From the hold of negativity,
As *Divinity* rises within my soul.
As new life unfolds within.

Earth, reborn.
Cleansed of sin.
Baptize my soul
In the *power of love.*
Ground my *Spirit* within
Her *soul*, and the
Universal stars above.

Galactic, I reform.
Essence of all life matter,
No longer shattered
Into pieces.
I Am whole.
I Am all things—

Risen from the depths
Of her oceans— Nourished.
Her *love* potion to heal your pain,
As she rebirths humanity
Again and again—
In the essence of *Divine Love.*

Pure Delight

O' Mystic Moon,
Not a day too soon,
As you reveal yourself
This night,

Pure ecstasy,
Is what my heart desires,
As you pour
Divine Radiance
Into my soul,
To deliver *Pure Delight*.

Quantum Force of Hate

Can the hearts of humanity
Be saved? Or will they rather take
Hate to their grave?
Lies spoken, as spells are broken,
Like the chains that set
Our ancestors free.

Because you are now
On America's soil,
You no longer have to toil
With your neighbors,
Over spoiled
Wastelands—
Cursed-infested battlefields
That continues to breed
Off-breeds of itself.

Dare you become hollow shells
For spirits to roam,
To claim your fleshly dominion
It's new home—
Now that is something to ponder,
As anguished souls wonder,
Preying on lost souls, such as hate,
As it becomes the *diminishing force*
It creates.

Rain Down Love

To the souls with
No name
We shall speak,
Itinerant voices—
Lost sheep.

Your voices rain high
To dimensions above,
To be cleansed of suffering,
With infinite love.

Speak not the meek,
As voices grow strong,
Nightmare lullabies',
Sing us a song.

Queen of all Queens,
Of our *Divine* world,
Take this wand
And give it a swirl.

1-2-3…
Repeat after me,
"Let there be love
For all humanity."

Rain down love
From my heavens,
Rain down love
To my oceans.

Love be unto thee,
Divine Energy.
Let there be *light.*
Let there be *love*—
Unto thy *Earth.*

Rebirth of thee I AM

Within the womb of thy sacred seas,
You carry the fertile essence of eternal life.
Along the *Nubian Nile,* you nourish thee—
Bringing all *Divine Beings* to life.

Sun Goddess, shine upon thy ambient face,
As I rebirth the *Essence* of thy *human race*—
All things are of thee.

Galactic crystals of thy beloved *Earth, Rebirthed,*
Into the likeness of thee *I AM. Compound,*
My fertile Earth. As I deliver thee— May you
Sustain the soul of humanity— To infinity.

Reflections of Love

As my *Earthly* oceans
Reflects the radiance
Of your *Universal* stars,
Absorbing all that you are—
Energize my pools
With *Divine* love.

Cosmic Universe's loving stars,
Etheric essence from abound,
In synchronicity with galaxies
Beyond my earthly realm,
Inspire all that *I AM*,
All that you are—

From afar, homing beacons
Of loving vibrations,
Reflections of Love.

Resonance of thee, I AM

An abundance of love
Flows through my essence
With each breath I take,
As my *Spirit* soar,
I shall rebirth my soul
Once more.

Incarnation of thy *Universe,*
Resonance of thee, *I Am,*
As I re-root my flesh
Upon thy *earthly* ground,
I shall not forsake thee.

As you nourish the soul
Within each inter-dimension
Of thy *Divine* skin,
I shall nourish the soul
Of humanity, in
The *Name of Love.*

Rhapsody of Love

Who are you—
Human mind,
To challenge the *creation of life,*
Divine Life;
Love.

Receive my love with gratitude.
The very fortitude
Of your being,
I bring to life!

Without *Divinity,*
To understand my energy,
Is a soul
Left to decay in misery.

The explosion of my soul
Captures the beauty
Of your essence,
As I explode in rhapsody—

Cosmic explosion of the
Spirit of the Universe—
Galaxies of love
From her heavens.

Rise of the Feminine Divine

Demonic possession
Of the human soul
Arose,
Warriors of the Great Spirit,
Defenders of Truth,
Justice, and *Humanity.*

Evil's War against itself
Is the worse sin of all,
As *Great Empires* rise and fall,
It shall give birth
To a new generation,
Much stronger than the last.

Sins of the past— Forgiven,
As cleansing
Of Earth's core begins.
She shall absorb all energy,
Good and *Bad*, for the purpose
Of healing herself.

As mankind wrestles
For power and dominion
Over oneself,
The Feminine Essence
Shall Rise,
Once again!!

Sage Beauty

The stillness of thy
Morose pond,
Majestically cascades
Your *Sage Beauty*,
During your most
Delicate season of
Fermentation,
Transmutation,
Manifestation
Of the rebirth
Of Divine life.

As thy healing waters
Preserves your soul,
May you continue to nourish
Generations to come.

Sands of Time

Destiny's ultimate fate with the *Grim Reaper*
  Meets its day of judgement
When hate no longer satisfies the desire
  Of the human soul—
The untimely death of what we create.

Mirrored reflections of the soul,
  Shattered at the glimpse of shame—
Shadowed embodiment of life form
  With no name.

Energy manifested into the being
  Of human life— Strife between
Dimensional realms of reality;
  Fragmented pieces of the *Divine* soul.

Dare you attempt to fit the pieces
  Back together again.
As reflections of your sins
  Stare into the scorned eyes of hate.

How loosely we carry life
  In our hands, like the *sands of time*—
Everyone must keep their appointment
  With the *Divine*, to rest in *Heaven;*
Earth's paradise.

Seeds of Divine Love

Love—
The flower
That blossoms
In a fertile soul,
Nourished
By the *Divine Essence*
Of a compassionate
Human Being.

Seeded—
In its most
Delicate state,
That reaps
The abundance
Of *Love.*

Self-Pity

Suppressed emotions,
Gradually eats away
At the core of the soul.

Unwelcomed guilt,
Placed upon the heart
Tears it apart,
Bit by bit.

Grief.
Guilt.
Thoughts unspoken.
Emotions withheld.
Happiness joins misery
To dwell in *self-pity*.

Decades of suppressed lies
Eventually fades,
Exposing what's left
Of a soul-decayed.

Burdens placed upon the heart,
Sins committed in the past—
At last, finds its way to the light,
To see favor in the *Universe's* delight.

Shadowed Illusions of the Soul

Tall,
Dark,
Handsome—
Mirrored reflections
Of the soul.

Shadowed illusions.
Reality.
Beauty of the *Spirit*
As *Divine* life unfolds.

Layers
Upon layers,
Dimensions
Upon
Dimensions,
Recycle of all life
Begins
Within.

Shine

Different vibes
For different times,
I see your smile…
Shine

Essence of love
Envelope me.
Nourish me.
Shine on me…
Shine

Radiate your essence
Upon my face…
Shine

Shine your smile
Into my heart…
Shine

Solitude of thy Earth

Into the *Soul* of thy *Earth*
My *Spirit* shall flow,
As I reciprocate
Her *love* for my *Soul*—
As *Divinity* envelopes me
To preserve my flesh,
I shall thrive
To do my best;

I shall become one
With thy *Earth,*
As my *Soul* is rebirthed,
I shall stand alone
Upon her throne;

Divine pillar of life
Beneath my feet,
She lies still—
For my quill is my *staff,*
To guide other *like minds*
To the *Soul* of the *Divine,*
As they seek peace and solitude
To *thrive* upon thy *Earth.*

So Much Love to Give

Receive me, as *I AM*,
Your Grace. For I bow
To your *heavenly throne.*
In request, for you to erase
The transgressions
Of the built-up aggression
That has plagued thine
Inner soul. As more lies
Entwined within
The stem cells of humanity
Unfolds—
Cleanse thy hearts of sin,
In each dimension
Of thy beloved *Earth.*

Let not her *wrath*
Repent in *Karma,*
Which lives on
To infinity—
Let the *Loving Light*
Of *Your Divinity*
Resonate to the
Black Heavens above.

For the Gift of Love,
Is all I ask for,
As only *you can give—*
As I forgive
All transgressions
That has been committed
Upon thy *Earth—*
And shall close this chapter
Of your *Divine Rebirth.*
We shall meet here again,
On better terms,
For there's so much more
To learn—
And *So Much Love to Give.*

Soul House

Creative Art,
Is the exploratory canvas of life,
Allowing the *Spirit, Mind, Body*
And Soul's composition
To find perfect balance
To the over-exposure of
Modern-day strife.

Each component stands alone,
In its own unique earthly home,
But once mis-influenced by
The outside environment,
It will cause one or the other to roam.

Finding *Universal* balance within,
Is to not consider all you do or say
As *cardinal sin—*
The *Universe* is forgiving.
As she recreates life, each day,
She gives us a chance to begin, again.

Unlike the *Laws of Karma,*
She forgives and forgets.
As she absorbs all in-between,
Keep your *soul house* in balance
And don't commit acts
That you would later regret.

Soul of the Universe

Hear my thunder clap.
As my lightening
Pervades your soul.
Bold, you say you are,
As your very survival
Exists upon my *Earthly Star.*

Dare you anger my soul,
As you show her no respect.
You will soon regret
That you have awakened me,
The *Great Spirit* beyond your realm.

Soon you will meet your maker—
Universe, I AM.

Spirit Matter

As your ray of light
Leads me home,
Amongst luminous particles
Of *Divine Energy,*
My *Spirit* roams
Throughout all matter
Of your *Divine Earth.*

Rebirthed
Into your likeness,
We shall become
Replicas of *Divine Energy,*
Nourished by the *Sun.*

As we blanket thy *Earth*
In *Spirit Matter*,
We shall live as one
Divine light—
A sea of rainbows
In the sky.

As thy *Heavenly Moon*
Absorbs all matter
Within your *Divine Universe*,
Darkness, no longer
Veils the sky.

As humanity
Says good bye
To hate, loving
Divine Energy
We shall create;
Within our hearts
And souls, as new life
Unfolds, as *One.*

Spirit of the Great Mother

In but a single breath,
Your essence
Ignites our soul,
Divine life unfolds.

To fill our hearts
And minds with
Divine energy,
To cleanse Earth of strife,
And bring about unity.

As we live and thrive as one,
Upon your fruitful earth,
The *Spirit of the Great Mother*
You shall be rebirth.

As she guides us
To honor our brothers
And fathers—
They themselves
Shall do the same,
In the *Universe's*
Holy Name.

Spirit Wild

Voices cry out
in the *spirit wild*,
singing sweet cries
of freedom;

The melodic rhythm
of their harmonic chants
dances in the wind,
in synchronicity
with the *Universe;*

As she swirls
her creations
in a single breath,
nourishing and
giving life,
to all creative beings.

Stardust

Glitter thy *Earth*
With your stardust,
Make it rain
Divine Crystals
From thy
Heavenly Universe;

Shower thee
With energetic
Fragments
Of thy galaxies,
Divine Loving
Energy.

Suppressed Emotions

Compound emotions.
Suppressed emotions.
Harbored emotions.

Release me from this pain.

Unwind me.
Restore me.
Nourish me.

Remove this evil stain.

Allow my soul to soar
Once more,
As my emotions roar.

Divine Universe I call to you,
Rescue me from these emotions,
So I can be of better service— To you.

Surrender Your Will

As I bond your heart's center
With the essence of my *Divine Love,*
Below, In-between and Above,
Free your will to me—

Surrender,
In the name of *Love,*
For the sake of
Peace and harmony.

Unity is my frequency,
Love is my vibration,
Salvation begins within,
With compassion for thy *Earth,*
And all Angelic beings.

As I bond your hearts with my
Universal Essence,
Surrender your will,
In the name of *Love.*

Synergy

Love,
Peace,
Balance,
Is the *synergy*
I bestow upon thy *Earth.*

Harmonic vibrations
Of my creations,
As I infuse rebirth
Of thy *Earthly Stars.*

Reincarnated
Into the likeness
Of the *I Am,*
My *Earthly* ground,
Compound,
Solid as a rock—

Etheric temples of Divine Life.

Cleansed of
Chaotic strife,
Which no longer
Embodies the
Human soul.

Hollow shells
You are to me,
As the *Spirit*
Of Divine Love
Encapsulates
My *Earth,*
Loving Beings
You shall be.

Tear Drops From Heaven

Open up your heart to me,
As your *Spirit* draws me near.
Twin souls infused by passion,
Our solar auras are clear.

Divine Energy,
Crystalline fragments
Of my soulful *Earth.*
Rebirthed.

From the depths of my oceans,
I gift to thee,
A token of *Divine Love—*
Teardrops,
From my heavens above.

Temple of the Divine Soul

As you try to restrain my gift,
The *Universe* ordains my frequency
To shift, with the tides
That balances the seas—
All components of thy Earth
Exists within me.

Do not try to control me.
For my power is uncontrollable
Like the *Earth*,
Who gives birth with each thought
That comes to mind.

Eyes no longer blind to your illusions
Which has become a mere delusion
Of your own mastery—
For sorcery is simply trickery,
That is forbidden in the temple
Of the *Divine Soul.*

The Energy of Love

The energy of love
is much calmer
and peaceful
than hate,
it's as serene
as the *morning sun*,
as it greets
the vibrant meadows
of dandelions,
as they spread
their petals
to receive
the peaceful glow
of the *sun's*
radiant energy,
as it nourishes
its stem,
fortifies its
roots, and
reciprocates
the loving
energy of
Mother Earth
as she receives
the warmth
of her *sun,*
to nourish
her core,
providing
protection and
sustainability
to all of her creations,
once more.

The Fertile Essence of Divine Life

Love liberates the soul,
Is what I was once told,
As the *Divinity of Life*
Unfolds— within.

Multi-dimensions of matter,
Lies beneath our skin,
Organized as one body—
The perfect-blend.

Earthly Temples—
Pillars of *Divine Life.*
Our connection to the *underworld*
Exists within our daily lives;

Where chaos envelopes our souls.
Where sin seduces our minds.
Where hate controls our energy.
Where we are the reflection of ourselves.

Mirrored reflections
Of hollow beings—
Castaways from the
Divine Universe;

Warped in a combustion
Of atomic energy;
Dwarf Stars– Ghostly beings,
Inhabitants of thy *Earth;*

Seeking to be rebirthed
Into the likeness of the, *I AM.*
Who is said to be
The *Divine Creator of All Life.*

Yet human scientific theories
Has barely touched the surface
Of thy mystery.

To explore the true nature
Of *Divine Life*, you must
Travel beneath thy oceans,
To the pools of *Divine Love*—

To the center of thy sacred abode,
The mystic jewel of humanity—
To rediscover,
The Fertile Essence of You!

The sustainer of life,
Created upon thy Earthly Universe;

The Illusion of Life

Ghostly illusions of fantasy,
Confronts us every day.
Fabricated thoughts of reality,
Harbors within dark crevices
Of our minds.
Blinded by mirrored reflections
Of our souls— Voices silenced.

A menagerie of puppet figures,
Dangles on a string.
Clogged toed-stilts—
Extensions of our minds.
Strawman figures
For the puppeteer,
The master magician;
The Grand Wizard, of Oz,
Orchestrating the many
Faces of humanity.

The Sound of Poetry

The sound of poetry, soothes my pain,
as the energy of hate and chaos
recycles again.
There is no better refuge
from the minds of the insane,
in our modern-day world
that allows full grown adults
to prey on the innocence of
young-undeveloped boys and girls,
simply to cater to their sinful pleasures,
to add to their trophies
and abundant treasures.

In their circles,
where no other eyes can see,
young children are considered
a delicacy— A rite of passage.
Young fruitful nectar.
Not the nectar of the fermented vines,
wine, of courses, which is much better
for the soul, and the human heart.
Why must humanity part
from the teachings of the holy scriptures,
The Book of the Sages?

But who am I, but an ancient scribe,
who knows the on goings,
between the scholars, and their pages.
Pageboys, of course.
And the young girls who tend to the needs
of the old. Whose vibrant *Spirits*
and young energy, help to fill
their hollow souls, and soothe their pain,
to rejuvenate their souls again.
Yet the only thing that soothes my pain,
is the sound of poetry.

The Universe Above

Infused within my stem,
A wand to heal humanity;
Vocal cord of the *Universe,*
Her Essence, spoken through me.
Gifted with the *seed of life,*
As her harmonic vibrations
Nourishes my eternal soul—
Through my pen, tales of
Her greatness, shall be told;
Scribed on behalf of the
Heavenly Goddess of Love,
Yours truly,
The Universe, Above.

Think of Me

Surrender gracefully.
Don't resist me.
For *I Am, You.*
As you are I.
We are all things.

For who *am I,*
Remains a mystery.
Simply breath in
My loving grace
And think of me.
Universe, I AM.

Tomorrow

Evening sunset,
I bask in your glory.
Stories told.
Stories written.
Survived, the sands of time.

Evening's light
Of the moon's shadow,
Ignites my essence.
Lucid dreams, rouses me,
To travel to galaxies afar.

A *Ray of light*
Guides my *Spirit,*
As it reflects through
To the doorway of my soul.

The *Essence of Love,*
Pours into me at day break.
As your *Morning Glory*
Guides my pathway
To the stars.

For now,
I shall enjoy life on *Earth.*
Until we meet again.
Tomorrow.

Twice Forgiven

Blessed are the beings
Of thy beloved *Earth,*
As I rebirth your souls, again.
Twice forgiven of sin,
As deliverance of your
Peaceful *salvation* begins—
Allow the *Season of Love*
To usher its way in.

Twice born—
Risen this day,
Bow your heads and pray…

Be thankful
That I have decided
Not to avenge the wrath
That has been committed
Against me.

For the souls of humanity
Shall be saved
By deliverance of the *same kind,*
Whose eyes are not blind to
Salvation within.

Tyranny, No More

The arduous road to freedom,
I helped to pave.
Through the blood and sweat
Of my labors—
As an indigenous slave

Upon our shores,
They arrived with their boats;
Hunted like wild animals,
As nooses strangled our throats.

Herded and branded like cattle,
To be auctioned as slaves—
The arduous road to freedom,
I helped to pave.

Centuries of bondage.
Centuries of lies.
Centuries of war.
As my bloodline dies.

Generations born.
Generations lost.
Generations re-born.
Generations lost.

As freedom is only but
A breathe away,
Resist the hands of tyranny,
As slavery fades away!

United as a Nation

United as a nation,
Under the flag of *Love.*
Its banner stretches so high,
To the cosmic *Universe* above.

Below—
Love reigns.
Surviving centuries
Long past.
Victory, at last.

United, in the name of *Love,*
Peace and *Harmony.*

Universal Energy

Hail, to thee,
O' Great Mystery
Of the Black Moon.
I surrender
Thy soul to thee,
As I bow to your
Divine throne!

Cast your light
Within my heart,
To awaken
The *Divine Spark*
In me.

Divine Greatness,
I ground thy roots
To your majesty,
The essence of
Universal Energy.

Universal Law and Order

As *Universal Law and Order*
Forces itself upon thy Earth,
To balance the *Scales of Justice*,
May the *Jupiter Star* forever guide
Our rebirth, to find peace and love
Within our hearts and souls;

As more tales are told, to bring reckoning
Of our immoral sins. For today begins
A new day, to tell a happier story,
To generations to come— Of how the
Glory of the Sun, thou Divine Universe,
Balanced our loving beings, forever more.

Universe, I AM, Divinely Yours

My *Spirit* resonates with
Soulful Expressions
Of the many ways I can say,
"*I Love You,*"
With *Absolute Truth.*
As we become *One Soul,*
Living in *Peace* and *Harmony*
With the *Divine Universe.*

Universe, Rebirthed Again

As a *New Age of Enlightenment*
Come to past,
My *Divine Essence*
Will forever last.

For *I Am* many things,
And many things are of me;
As my *Essence* syncs
With thy beloved *Earth,*
To nourish the soul of humanity.

All *Divine* life shall be compound
To rebirthed the essence
Of thy *Earthly* ground—
The D*ivine Soul* of the *Universe, I Am.*

I Am the clap of the thunder's roar.
I Am the spark of the lightening's ore.
I Am the flow of the ocean's stream.
I Am the harp of the Universe's strings.
I Am the melody the Angels' sings.
I Am the hills of the mountain's peak.
I Am the soft cry of the meek.
I Am the strength of the souls that reign.
I Am the *Universe*, rebirthed again.

Vibration of Love

Everywhere you stop and stare,
My essence is everywhere.
All around and about
You'll see,
Remnants of my *Divine Energy*—

Auras,
Within auras.
Dimensions,
Within dimensions.

Void.
Time.
Space.
Unison.

All matter,
All sound,
All frequencies,
In sync
With my synergy.
The *Vibration of Love*

My pulse is the rhythm
That attunes
To your heart,
Bonding my love
To your soul—
No longer apart.

We shall dance
In unison as
One Sound,
One Vibration,
Love—

Feel my drums,
As I beat a new rhythm

Into your hearts.
For nothing,
(Not even hate)
Shall tear us apart!

As we dance in cadence
With the *Universe,*
I shall resonate thee,
To become one with me,
Loving, *Divine Energy.*

Our love is compound—
Within thy *Earth,*
Within thy *Universe,*
Within thy *Stars,*
Within thy *Soul.*
For we are One Soul.

As *Truth* of the *I Am*
Unfolds the pages of time,
To reveal the essence of
The *Universal Divine,*
There shall be no more scriptures
To speak *untruths* of me.
Awakening within your soul
Is your connection
to my *Divine Essence.*

All flesh,
All bodies,
All temples,
You shall be—
As my *Spirit*
Guides your inner soul
To the heights of *Divinity;*

My energy shall nourish
All human minds.
Humanity,
No longer blind
To my *All.*

For you shall be as, *I Am,*
As, *I Am,* of you.

I shall guide your thoughts
With reflections of all that you do.
For you shall carry
The *Vibration of Love*
With each word you speak.

You shall inspire
The hearts of the meek,
And the strength
Of the weak.

I shall awaken your hearts
To the power of love within,
To heal the soul of humanity
Once again.

Warriors of Divine Love

There's no victory in misery.
When the dust settles,
All that's left to celebrate
Is a ravished *Earth,*
Who simply seeks to rebirth
Divine Love.

Seeds of eternal life
Shall become sewn
When love becomes the
Ultimate sacrifice—
To surrender to hate,
The collective masses of the
Forces we now create.

Negative energy that compels
The heart, when forced to part,
Resonates with the *High GOD's,*
Whose rods shall not strike
But the might of their will
Shall preserve thy *Earth,*
As she remains still
During times of adversity.

Preservation of humanity
Is the duty of us all, and
We shall not befall
To hateful energy,
As we evolve into Warriors
Of *Divine Loving Energy.*

Waterfalls

Rainbow Essence of the Divine,
Cosmic glitter of *gold,*
Rubies, diamonds, and pearls.

Beautifully swirled
Crystalline fragments
Of your aura,
As new life unfolds—
Reflections of your *Earthly* soul.

Cascading waterfalls of heaven,
As your glory rain down
Into the rivers—
You shall be the silver
Thread, to mend *my* broken soul.

Welcome to My Queendom

Welcome to my *Queendom*,
Where I allow your *Spirit* to soar.
Where I enchant you with ecstasy,
Where all pleasures are adored,
And new realms are explored.

What is your fantasy?
What is your desire?
What is your request?,
As I ignite your lustful fire.

I shall guide you to the light within,
To satisfy all *Cardinal Sins,*
As your *Spirit* takes flight,
Into my *Queendom* this night,
I shall fulfill the delights
Of your fantasies,
Where my *Heavens*
Rouses your eyes to see,
Lust,
Temptation,
Seduction—
Divine Energy.

When

When is the *World*
going to *Rise Up*
against *Hate*?

When is the *World*
going to realize that
We are what we create.

When is the *World*
going to move *forward*,
to write a new
scripture in life?

When is the *World*
going to *Unite,*
in Love— Not *strife*?

When is the *World*
going to *forgive, and erase*
all of its sins?

When is the *World*
going to welcome *Love*
into their hearts again?

Hate has a way of
eating at the core
of the human soul.

Hate has a way of
resurrecting the *old,*
and making room
for the *new.*

Love *(not hate)*
should be a reflection of
what we *Say* and *Do*!

L - O - V - E
Evolve with me,
to love and embrace
LOVE!

Where Dreams Come True

Take me to a world unknown.
Take me to a world of fantasy.
Take me to a world
Where dreams come true.
A world built by me and you.
    Illusions
    Fantasy
    Reality
A world where dreams come true.

Womb of Love

There is a realm that exists
Far beyond my head,
I dread
To follow the path to its existence.
Its origin.

I've been told
It's a sin
To think beyond
The ordinary thoughts of mankind,
Whose eyes are blind to the reality
Of the creation of *Divinity.*

Her *Universal Laws* does not exists
In his world—
Mere fabrications of illusions
of magic— *Hocus Pocus*
Of old witches brew.

In a kingdom of darkness
Where the celestial realms creates
And feeds off its own energy,
Is the *Divine* realm
Where all life co-exists
Within her *Womb of Love.*

Wrinkle in Time

(Dedicated to the legacy of Michael Jackson)

If there was ever a *Wrinkle in Time*,
I wish I could erase,
It would be to dissolve
The countless lies
That's been told about you,
So *Heaven* can find you space.

So many words you've written,
To describe how you feel,
And the composition of your
Timeless melodies,
Shall reinforce a heart of steel.

As time, never truly heal
Old wounds, as more acid
Is poured onto your soul,
May your *Spirit* soar
To the depths of the *Universe*,
Who shall release your curse.

As your legacy is restored,
And all curses are lifted,
Be the guiding like from above
To always inspire the gifted.

X-Mas in My Heart

Let us be joyful and merry
All of the time, as we sip wine—
Toasting, in celebration of the good life;
When everyday feels like *X-Mas.*

When giving the gift of *Love,*
Compassion and *Respect,*
Goes a long way.

When a positive attitude,
Thoughts, Mantras,
Salutations—
Simply giving from the heart
While expecting nothing in return,
Are kind deeds worth celebrating.

You Are Love

You are love.
You are *Divine Light*
From the heavens above.
You're the angel of my eye.
You are the depths
To my rising seas—
You nourish *Divine Life*
Inside of me.
You are Love.

Zenith is My Reality

When I reflect back
On the road I've traveled
To get here, I do not fear
The thought of

Reaching a little higher…
Dreaming a bit bigger…
And grounding my Spirit
To the Soulful Essence of
The Universe—

In hopes of a more loving
And compassionate rebirth.
That my incarnation will be
Better than the last.

Zenith is my reality,
As Infinity becomes my
Next destination,
To capture and embrace
The galactic sensation of
Love.

Love…
The Beauty of All Life forms.

www.ingramcontent.com/pod-product-compliance
Lightning Source LLC
Chambersburg PA
CBHW070552160426
43199CB00014B/2478